THE ANIMALS' WISHES

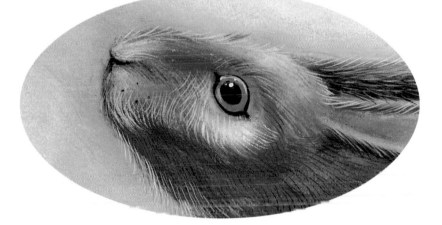

DOVIE THOMASON

ILLUSTRATED BY
BEE WILLEY

*This is a traditional Native American tale
about the rabbil and the owl
and how they came to be like they are today.*

Rigby

Long, long ago when the world was young, and some animals were still to be made, the Maker decided to give these creatures a say in their own features. If their wishes were good ones, they were granted.

One day a small, unfinished ball of fur came rolling along. The Maker gently put it on a log.

"So, Little One, what do you need?"

"I would like ears, so I can listen for danger."

"To want to listen is a
good thing. You may have
your ears," smiled the Maker.

5

"What else do you need?"

"I would like long legs to run away from danger!"

"To avoid trouble is a good thing. You may have your long legs. What else do you need?"

Suddenly a sharp squawk pierced the air.

"HEY! What about ME?" a shapeless ball of feathers screeched from a nearby tree. "I want red, shiny feathers, strong wings to fly all day and night, a lon-n-n-n-n-g neck like a swan, and a sweet song to sing! And I want them NOW!"

The Maker frowned.

"Who are you who interrupts?
It is not your turn. Look away,
Noisy One."

The Maker spoke to the Little One again. "I'm sorry. Is there anything else you need?"

The Little One looked up shyly. "Could I possibly have a long silky tail — just because it's pretty?"

The Maker nodded.

"The Earth needs beauty in all her
children. You may have your tail."

And so, the Maker set to work.
First, he gently gathered some fur
on either side of the Little One's
head, to make two tall ears.

Next, the Maker pulled two long, powerful hind legs down from the Little One's body.

Then he started work on the front legs in the same way. But before he could stretch them out, he was interrupted again . . .

"**HEY**! What about **ME**?
I want red, shiny feathers, strong
wings to fly all day and night,
a lon-n-n-n-n-g neck like a swan,
and a sweet song to sing! And I'm
tired of waiting!"

The Maker was growing impatient. "I told you not to watch!" he said. "You speak too much of what you *want*, and nothing of what you *need*. Turn away, Noisy One, and wait until I'm ready!"

Now the Maker had completely
forgotten what he was doing.
"Oh yes — beauty," he murmured.
He gathered fur together on the
Little One's back, but before
he could stretch it into a long,
silky tail . . .

"HEY! What about ME?
I want red, shiny feathers, strong
wings to . . ."

"You, AGAIN . . ." The Maker spun toward the tree, his voice like thunder. "I will give you what you need. I told you to turn away, and I shall make you do so!"

And reaching out, he twisted the feathered head right around.

The Noisy One's eyes bulged with surprise.

"I won't give you red feathers because then you would be hard to ignore. You will be the colors of the Earth, so you remember that you are only one of her many children."

And the Maker smeared streaks and stripes of clay all over its feathers.

"You may have your wings, but they will be silent night wings. I work in the day," said the Maker, "and I don't want to be interrupted."

"I won't make your neck
as long as a swan's because then
you'd never keep your beak out
of anyone's business. So I won't
give you a neck at all."

And the Maker tapped on the
Noisy One's head, until it rested
between its shoulders.

"I will give you a song but it will be only one word. You don't listen well enough to learn a longer song," explained the Maker. "Your song will be . . . WHO . . .

WHO . . .

WHO . . ."

And that is why Owl is as he is today. Owl learned his lesson and has never forgotten WHO he interrupted. Since that time, Owl glides through the night on silent wings.

Seeing all this, the startled Little One tried to run away. But her hind legs were too long and they folded beneath her body — so she could only hop!

And to this day, poor Rabbit always looks frightened because she can hear danger, but knows she cannot run. All because of Owl.

And Rabbit *is* being followed! But only by a puff of a tail . . .